Original title:
Propagating Peace

Copyright © 2025 Creative Arts Management OÜ
All rights reserved.

Author: Julian Prescott
ISBN HARDBACK: 978-1-80581-826-7
ISBN PAPERBACK: 978-1-80581-353-8
ISBN EBOOK: 978-1-80581-826-7

The Healing Touch of Kindness

In a world where grumps often roam,
A smile can lead them back home.
With cookies baked, all warm and sweet,
Offer one, now that's a treat!

When life gets tough and humor's rare,
A wave can lighten loads we bear.
Tell a joke or share a pun,
Laughter's light, a life well done!

A hug's like magic, soft and warm,
It melts away the fiercest storm.
With goofy hats, let's dance around,
In silliness, joy's always found!

In kindness, mischief often grows,
A nod, a wink, the fun just flows.
So let's unite, don't be a grouch,
Come join the game, on kindness' couch!

The Roots of Understanding

In the garden of chatter, we plant a few seeds,
Digging deep, pulling weeds, no one's in need.
With laughter we water, our smiles take flight,
Growing bonds through the day, and high fives at night.

The critters join in with their quirky surprise,
A squirrel on a trampoline, spreading good vibes.
In this patch of goodwill, the sun shines so bright,
We're all silly farmers, from morning till night.

Kindred Spirits in Motion

Two ducks on a pond, sharing tales of their days,
They waddle and quack in their own funny ways.
With every splash made, they stir up a cheer,
Bumping into each other, no room for a sneer.

The fish flip and giggle, joining the fun,
A circle of joy that's never outrun.
In this dance of delight, we're all part of the show,
With splashes and laughter, we let our hearts glow.

Blossoms of Bridged Differences

From daisies to dandelions, a colorful crew,
With petals and puns, we're waving at you!
We play hopscotch on differences, laughing out loud,
Each bloom tells a tale, unique and proud.

In the wind's silly stories, we all take a spin,
The pollen of friendship makes us all grin.
So let's toss out the tension, like confetti in air,
And join in the laughter, with colors to share.

Serene Horizons

On the edge of a sunset, with friends all around,
We tumble and roll on this soft grassy ground.
The sky paints our dreams in a riotous hue,
And we giggle like kids when the stars peek through.

With jokes and tall tales, we stretch out our hands,
Creating a haven where no one demands.
As night blankets softly, we whisper with glee,
In this sea of delight, we're forever carefree.

Strands of Unity Woven Tight

In a world where socks all roam,
Woven threads find a place called home.
Birds and bees dance in a line,
Sharing snacks and sipping wine.

Mutts and moggies play all day,
Chasing tails in a cheerful way.
Laughter jingles like a bell,
Unity's secret, can't you tell?

When the sun sets, friends unite,
Under stars, oh what a sight!
Cosmic giggles fill the night,
Togetherness feels just right.

With each twist of fate we weave,
Crazy patterns we believe.
Hand in hand with hearts aglow,
Creating joy wherever we go.

A Chorus of One

In a land where cats can sing,
Every purr's a joyful thing.
Dogs join in, but with a bark,
As harmony ignites a spark.

The cows provide a bass so low,
While the roosters steal the show.
Together they make quite a sound,
Bringing joy all around town.

A duck quacks jokes, the sheep all cheer,
While goats roll on, no room for fear.
With each note that fills the air,
Laughter blooms without a care.

So join the fun, don't be shy,
Let your spirit soar and fly.
In this choir, you'll find your place,
Singing songs of love and grace.

Tides of Change and Compassion

Waves of giggles crash the shore,
As jellyfish dance, not a bore.
Starfish throw a beach ball high,
Underneath the sunny sky.

Crabs wear shells, a fashion show,
With a swagger, they steal the flow.
Sand castles rise, then tumble down,
In this sea of smiles, no frown.

Surfboards glide on sea of dreams,
With dolphins sharing silly schemes.
Together they ride the wild spray,
Compassion waves, come out and play.

As tides pull back, we gather round,
With each laugh, a friendship found.
Commit to joy, let troubles cease,
In this ocean, find your peace.

The Heartbeat of Humanity

A squirrel with a tiny drum,
Beating rhythms, oh so fun!
Rabbits hop to the clever beat,
In this realm, they can't be beat.

Frogs croak tunes, a grand affair,
While turtles dance without a care.
Even ants march in their shoes,
Creating paths we can't refuse.

Laughter echoes through the trees,
Like a gentle autumn breeze.
With each bump and silly fall,
Hearts draw closer, one and all.

So join the band, don't hold back,
Find your groove on this great track.
With every pulse and every sway,
Together we'll laugh and play.

Borders of the Soul

In a land where ducks wear crowns,
We laugh at the silly towns.
With hats on goats and shoes on cats,
Joy spreads, just like welcome mats.

Silly dances to wacky tunes,
Juggling rabbits and wooden spoons.
We paint rainbows with giggles bright,
And tickle the stars every night.

Building Foundations of Trust

Like squirrels tossing acorns high,
We share our snacks—oh my, oh my!
With high-fives flying, friendship blooms,
And cookie crumbs scatter in rooms.

We trust that pie will always share,
In every laugh, there's love laid bare.
From giggles stout to whispers sweet,
Joy hangs around like a cozy seat.

A Mosaic of Hope

In jellybean colors, hope does thrive,
Creating rainbows where we jive.
With bows and arrows made of light,
We're artists of laughter, what a sight!

Patchwork dreams sewn with a grin,
Each thread a smile, it's where we begin.
With silly hats and wands all bright,
Let's dance together, hearts taking flight.

Currents of Kinship

In rivers of jelly, we shall swim,
With penguins laughing on a whim.
Tickling waves that hug the shore,
Together we giggle, wanting more.

Frogs croaking tunes under the moon,
They sing to friends, all too soon.
With wave-like hugs and whispers soft,
We find our kinship, lifting us aloft.

Luminescence of Shared Visions

In a world where giggles bloom,
We share our crumbs and clear the room.
When joys collide, we dance and sway,
A chain of laughter lights our way.

With silly hats and shoes askew,
We find the bonds that hold us true.
In every joke that we declare,
We stitch our hearts with threads of care.

With every pun that makes us smile,
We bridge the gap, we go the mile.
In this bright game of give and take,
Every chuckle is a splendid wake.

So here's to fumbles and good cheer,
Together we can shift the sphere.
In this bright world where spirits rise,
Our shared delight is the grand prize.

The Togetherness Effect

A cupcake here, a cookie there,
We gather treats, a tasty affair.
With friends around to share the load,
We spin our tales down this sweet road.

A sprinkle here, a frosting fight,
We chase the towers of sugar's height.
Who knew the bond of crumbs and cream,
Could weave together such a dream?

In laughter's sway, we find our place,
With frosting smiles and silly grace.
We catch the joy in every snort,
As friendships bloom in sugar's court.

So let's embrace this merry vibe,
Hold hands and join this tasty tribe.
With every bite and every cheer,
We build our bubble, loud and clear.

A Garden of Gentle Intent

In a garden bright with giggles loud,
We plant our hopes beneath a cloud.
With playful seeds of kindness sown,
We water dreams; we're never alone.

A ripple of joy, a splash of fun,
Dancing daisies greet the sun.
As butterflies flit from bloom to bloom,
We stir the air—no room for gloom.

With wiggly worms that wiggle tight,
The soil turns soft, a pure delight.
With every sprout, a heart expands,
In this sweet patch, we join our hands.

So grab a spade, let's turn the earth,
In every smile, we find our worth.
Through laughter's light, the garden grows,
A cheerful patch where love just flows.

The Harmony of Many Voices

A chorus of chuckles fills the air,
With silly songs that we all share.
We hum a tune, we strum a beat,
In wobbly lines, we dance on feet.

From high-pitched notes to whispers low,
Our laughter's symphony begins to flow.
A cacophony of friendly glee,
We harmonize like birds, carefree.

In crooked lines like butterflies,
We flip and flop to joyful highs.
With every lyric, we lift our hands,
Creating magic, heart expands.

So let's combine our voices true,
With silly riffs, a whole new crew.
In this bright world where laughter sings,
Together we create such wondrous things.

The Embrace of Different Souls

In a world of quirks and puzzles,
We all dance in our own huddles.
A goat in boots and a cat with ties,
Team up to spread giggles and sighs.

Bringing together all kinds of folks,
With laughter that doubles as soothing jokes.
A baker with dreams of unicorns sweet,
And a juggler with pies for a funny treat.

United we stand, a colorful crew,
Each soul a shade of a vibrant hue.
With puns at the ready and smiles galore,
Our differences melt like ice on the floor.

So let's spin tales of harmony loud,
Amidst howling laughter, we gather a crowd.
In the embrace of our wacky array,
Together we'll dance, come what may.

The Lighthouse of Forgiveness

Once a lighthouse shone bright and proud,
With beams of light that danced like a crowd.
But one little bulb had trouble, they say,
It flickered often and led boats astray.

The sailor sighed, "Oh what can I do?
How to fix this light that's making me blue?"
But the lighthouse chuckled, "Just give me a chance,
I'll shine through your troubles with a merry romance."

With humor as bright as the sun in July,
The sailor learned not to give up and cry.
For mistakes are just giggles wearing a frown,
And love's the quick fix when you're feeling down.

So let's all be lighthouses, bright and clear,
Shining our beams through troubles and fear.
With laughter and light, we'll navigate right,
Forgiveness will guide us, our hearts in full sight.

Gentle Murmurs of Solidarity

In the quiet of night, whispers take flight,
A chorus of mice sings a tune of delight.
With tiny paws tapping in time with the beat,
They spread out their hopes with each little tweet.

From crowded rooftops to meadows so vast,
Their giggles carry, a sweet little cast.
Each murmur a promise to share in the fun,
No rivalries here, just the warmth of the sun.

Together they plot to bake cupcakes bright,
Sugary dreams on a whimsical night.
With sprinkles as flags and frosting as cheer,
Their solidarity bubbles, and laughter draws near.

So join in the whispers, let your heart join the song,
For in gentle murmurs, we all can belong.
With kindness as icing on our little cake waits,
Let's giggle together while opening our gates.

The Journey of Joining Hands

Two clowns on a unicycle, taking a ride,
Their balance is wobbly, but joy's on their side.
With hands held together, they giggle and sway,
Making fumbles a part of their playful display.

Through laughter-filled streets and puddles galore,
They hop over giggles, and call for more.
Each misstep is met with a cheeky embrace,
For the road is much better when shared in this race.

With a jingle of bells and a rattle of spoons,
They serenade friends under glowing balloons.
From the tallest of swings to the tiniest hand,
They build up their dreams on this laughter-filled land.

So let's take a lesson from jokesters so brave,
That the journey is better when we learn how to wave.
With hands intertwined, we'll glide and we'll dance,
In this whimsical life, be open to chance.

River of Togetherness

In the river of laughter, we all splash,
Floating our worries, making a dash,
With rubber ducks bobbing, we find our way,
Who knew peace could be this fun to play?

Fishing for giggles, we cast our line,
Each catch a joke, oh isn't it fine?
We build tiny boats from gossip and cheer,
As we sail on trust, not a worry or fear.

Splashing around, we dance in delight,
Making waves of joy, hearts feeling light,
In this river, no frowns or woes,
Just a friendly tide where laughter flows.

Silhouettes of Cooperation

In the glow of twilight, we dance on a wall,
Shadows spinning swiftly, who'll trip and fall?
Arm in arm, we create quite a sight,
Dancing together, we're clumsy but bright.

Lending a hand feels like magic tonight,
Like juggling watermelons, oh what a sight!
With every misstep we chuckle and grin,
In our silly ballet, the fun's about to begin.

Just like a puzzle with pieces so weird,
Together we fit, and nobody's feared,
As silhouettes whisper, "We've got this, my friend,"
In cooperation's dance, the laughter won't end.

The Garden of Friendship

In a garden of giggles, we plant every seed,
Watering joy with kindness, that's all that we need,
Sunshine and laughter, our flowers all bloom,
Who knew that in chaos, there's always more room?

We grow green thumbs from helping each other,
Weeds of doubt vanish, like magic they smother,
With trowels of trust and shovels of play,
Our roots intertwine, no reason to sway.

Snacking on fruits of tremendous delight,
Sharing our harvest each whimsical night,
In this garden of friendship, love plants the seeds,
Watered with laughter, fulfilling our needs.

Tides of Compassion

As the tide rolls in, with a whoosh and a swell,
We surf on kindness, oh can't you tell?
With surfboards of hope and a beachball of care,
Each wave brings a smile, floating joy in the air.

Building sandcastles made of good deeds,
With every grain shared, our friendship proceeds,
The ocean laughs back, it's a merry old game,
In the tides of compassion, we're all in the same frame.

Riding the currents, we splash and we cheer,
For in these warm waters, there's nothing to fear,
As we collect seashells of moments so bright,
Together we dance in the soft moonlight.

Threads Woven in Grace

In a garden where giggles grow,
Laughter seeds in a friendly row.
A cat in a hat gives a little wink,
While neighbors share cookies and lemonade drink.

A squirrel debates with a wise old crow,
Who'll win the nut prize? It's hard to know.
Dancing daisies announce with style,
That being silly makes life worthwhile.

The sun spills joy on each passing face,
As everyone joins in the silly chase.
With high-fives flying left and right,
We stitch our stories with pure delight.

So let's spread smiles like butterflies,
And embrace the laughs, oh what a prize!
In this swirling world, so wonderfully odd,
We'll dance together, giving a nod.

A Symphony of Hope

An orchestra tunes with ducks and geese,
Playing quacks and honks, such a fun release.
A cow on trombone, with rhythm divine,
Agriculture's band, all hearts intertwine.

The sheep bring a beat, oh so fabulous,
While cats on the piano play notes contagious.
With hearts like instruments, we take the stage,
Creating a melody that breaks every cage.

In harmony, we twirl like spinning tops,
Each note is a hug, and we never stop.
A cacophony of chuckles fills the air,
As laughter and love soundtrack everywhere.

So let the world dance to this silly tune,
Under the whimsy of the afternoon.
Together, we'll jam until stars are bright,
A symphony of hope, shining the night.

Under the Same Sky

Two friends on swings, side by side,
With clouds as their audience, filled with pride.
They swap funny tales of their comical flaws,
While ants on parade break out in applause.

A kite gets tangled, oh what a sight,
As neighbors all giggle, "Let's give it a fight!"
They pull it together, it soars with glee,
Under the same sky, we're all family.

With paper planes gliding through the blue,
And laughter that echoes in every hue,
The sun joins the fun, tickling our toes,
As joy multiplies wherever it goes.

So wave at the stars, and don't be shy,
For dreams are best shared, oh me, oh my!
Together we roam this beautiful playground,
Under the same sky, our laughter resounds.

The Canvas of Coexistence

With brushes of kindness, we splash and we play,
Creating a mural that brightens the day.
The colors unite in a goofy parade,
As giggles and chuckles in harmony wade.

A polka-dotted elephant likes to dance,
While a zebra in stripes takes a silly chance.
They twirl round the canvas, with colors galore,
Showing the world that we crave to explore.

A portrait of hugs and a masterpiece of cheer,
Sprays of confetti bring the whole town near.
With laughter as pigments, together we blend,
In this artwork of life, let the fun never end!

So grab a paintbrush, come join in the cheer,
Let's make this a canvas that's loved and sincere.
Unified colors, hand in hand embrace,
Creating a gallery full of grace.

A Symphony of Understanding

In the land where giggles grow,
A parrot cracks a wise old joke.
The trees sway, wiggling in cheer,
While flowers bloom with a friendly poke.

Bees debate on who's the best,
As ants march in a funky line.
The caterpillars get some rest,
Dreaming of their dance next time.

A squirrel shimmies on a branch,
Offering nuts with a goofy smile.
The world's a stage, a silly chance,
For laughter to go the extra mile.

Together we jam, a joyful tune,
Harmony in every little note.
With silly hats, we hum at noon,
In this symphony, let's all gloat.

Threads of Tranquility

A lion wears a knitted scarf,
While turtles spin in leisure's thread.
Each stitch a tale, a hearty laugh,
Knitting peace where once was dread.

The rabbits hop, making chains,
Bouncing high with goofy grace.
They tie their tales in playful reins,
Laughing as they join the race.

A spider weaves with a twinkling eye,
Creating webs that sparkle bright.
With each loop, a little lie,
Of how the moon still shines at night.

The owl hoots with a tip-top hat,
Sipping tea in the evening glow.
Binding us in this, imagine that,
Threads of laughter start to flow.

The Garden of Compassion

In a garden where jokes bloom wide,
A pumpkin and a cucumber dance.
With leaves that rustle, side by side,
They create a sweet merry prance.

Petunias giggle with every breeze,
While daisies shake, they can't keep still.
The sunflowers twirl; they aim to please,
Spreading laughter with winter's chill.

A busy bee with a funny hat,
Buzzes 'round with comic flair.
Even the worms are chuckling at,
The wiggle dance they choose to share.

Under the moon's soft, bright glee,
We gather for a rainbow feast.
With veggies both funny, and quite free,
Compassion blooms as we laugh the least.

Echoes of Unity

In a park where giggles collide,
A parade of critters takes the stage.
With frogs and owls, side by side,
Their silly antics write the page.

A monkey swings with a cheeky grin,
While crickets chirp a lullaby tune.
Together they dance, and we all join in,
Under the glow of a shiny moon.

A raccoon wears a polka dot tie,
While hedgehogs spin in a wild race.
With joy that hums, they reach for the sky,
Unity blooms in this funny space.

The night ends with a ticklish cheer,
As laughter hops from ear to ear.
In every heart, a little sphere,
Of unity that's oh-so-clear.

Threads of Concord

In a room full of laughter, we share a big pie,
Everyone gets a slice, but why not the sky?
With each little giggle, a knot starts to weave,
Stitching up troubles that no one believes.

When the cat starts to dance and the dog steals a sock,
Unity bubbles, it flows like a rock.
We're all just strange birds on a wild, breezy shore,
Singing silly anthems, always hungry for more.

Jokes bounce like bubbles, some land on a head,
Laughter is glue that can never be shed.
In this circus of life, we juggle the light,
Tossing frowns in the air, till they dance out of sight.

So bring your own quirks, and let's make a fuss,
Together we'll blur lines on the big golden bus.
With hearts wide as oceans and spirits that soar,
Let's craft a bright tapestry—who could ask for more?

Blossoms of Calm

A tickle of sunshine, a dash of sweet jam,
Sprinkled with giggles, it's more than a plan.
Petals flapping wildly, like birds on a spree,
Every bloomin' chuckle becomes part of our tea.

We toss silly hats on a very tall tree,
And watch with delight as birds argue with glee.
The squirrels think we're nuts, but that's all to the good,
We're crafting a garden where laughter's understood.

Tea parties with crumpets, or socks in a race,
Every moment's a gift, every smile's an ace.
With shoes made of giggles, and hearts full of zest,
In this patch of pure humor, we're all at our best.

So come dance in the daisies, the world's feeling bright,
With joy that outshines every shadow in sight.
Let's paint our adventure in colors so grand,
With flowers of whimsy, we're never unsanned!

Hummingbird's Embrace

A hummingbird darts by with a wink and a whirl,
Buzzing through fun, like a quirky little girl.
She sips on the nectar, oh, isn't she spry?
In this garden of giggles, she swoops and she flies.

Each question a riddle, each answer a cheer,
A playful exchange, where no one feels fear.
We dance in the symphony, music in play,
Mixing sweet laughter with a hint of ballet.

Like kite strings entangled, we float up so high,
Chasing the sun as we dance through the sky.
Though life may be tricky, with leaps and with bounds,
We'll glide hand in hand, where the joy always sounds.

So let's savor this moment, drink deeply of cheer,
With kindness our anchor and laughter our pier.
In this garden of fun, we've stitched our own lace,
Every smile a treasure, in the hummingbird's embrace.

Melodies of Understanding

In the symphony of life, we're jamming a tune,
With kazoos and tambourines, beneath the bright moon.
We'll harmonize giggles, on clouds made of fluff,
Playing silly solos when the going gets tough.

As we march through the park in a polka-dot line,
We send out our joy—just like a big sign.
With banjos and ukes, we create a parade,
Making friends with the cats who rest in the shade.

Each note's like a tickle—oh, laughter's contagious,
Dancing like fireflies, feeling quite outrageous.
We'll strum on our dreams, through the hills and the trees,

With belly laughs ringing out, filling whispers with ease.

So gather your quirks, bring your joy to the game,
In the melodies we craft, not a heart feels the same.
United we revel, as silly as can be,
In this concert of oneness, come sing along with me!

Gentle Hands, Strong Hearts

With gentle hands we bake a pie,
A recipe for smiles piled high.
Mix in some laughter, a pinch of cheer,
A slice to share, bring everyone near.

Let's juggle kindness, toss it 'round,
Like rubber chickens, joy is found.
When we lift each other, oh what a sight,
Hearts dance together, oh what delight!

Tie-dye shirts on a sunny spree,
Our hearts beat strong, wild and free.
With hugs like pillows and jokes that soar,
Let's be the team that everyone adores!

So hand in hand, with quirk and glee,
We paint our world, just wait and see.
A funny dance, a goofy grin,
Together as one, let the fun begin!

The Flame of Mutual Respect

A flicker here, a sparkle there,
We light the way with good old flair.
Balloons of kindness, they float so high,
Inflated with giggles, they touch the sky.

When differences sway like funky tunes,
We clap our hands, we dance like loons.
With silly hats and mismatched socks,
We build a bond that truly rocks!

Turn the spotlight on a giant cake,
Each slice a story, the memories we make.
With frosting smiles and cherry cheers,
We conquer doubts and erase fears.

So pass the torch and let it glow,
Together we shine, come on let's go!
With fires of friendship lighting the way,
We'll chuckle and chortle every day!

Whispers of Empathy

In the quiet corners of this big old room,
Whispers of kindness break the gloom.
A wink, a nod, a tickle or two,
Empathy giggles, sharing with you.

Float like clouds on a cotton candy day,
We troll through troubles and frolic and play.
With silly jokes and a gentle tease,
We soothe each other, life's little breeze.

High-five the sun, let's wave to the moon,
Mirth is a language, we chat in tune.
With chuckles that echo and laughter that rings,
Each whisper we share is joy that it brings.

So let's take a stroll, arm in arm,
With jests like umbrellas, shielding from harm.
Together we giggle, a mirthful spree,
In this symphony of joy, close as can be!

Unity in Diversity

With crayons in hand, let's start to draw,
A world where differences fill us with awe.
Rainbow butterflies and polka-dot cows,
In our quirky garden, we'll take a bow!

Let's mix our flavors, sweet and zesty,
Tacos and sushi, isn't that testy?
Every dish tells a story, oh so grand,
In this banquet of laughs, all hand in hand.

Wiggle our way through cultures galore,
Dance with a cat, moonwalk on the floor.
In every step, we find shades of light,
Unity blooms, making wrongs feel right.

So lift a toast, let the laughter flow,
In this epic party, everyone's in the show!
With hearts wide open and smiles so bright,
Let's shout out our joys throughout the night!

Reflections of Forgiveness

A bird dropped a sandwich, oh what a sight,
The ants had a feast, quite a delight!
Forgiving the bird for its messy snack,
In a world full of crumbs, there's nothing we lack.

Lemonade spilled on a sidewalk so neat,
A child laughed hard, losing their seat.
Forgiveness is sweet like that sugary drink,
Making fun out of mishaps, don't you think?

A cat chased a laser, zooming about,
But tripped on a rug and gave a loud shout!
With a twitch of its tail, it just couldn't win,
Laughter erupted, it just had to grin!

So here's to the blunders we often make,
In the garden of life, it's joy we will stake.
With giggles and chuckles, we'll dust off the past,
Forlife's too amusing to let sour thoughts last.

The Light in Each Heart

A candle in daylight, barely a glow,
But when night falls, watch how it'll show!
Each heart has its spark, a twinkle or two,
Together we shine, like a disco ball crew.

A cat in a bowtie, charming and sly,
Winks with a purr, sends a sweet hi!
Every soft chuckle, a flicker of cheer,
In the orchestra of life, let's give a loud cheer!

Bananas on skateboards, banana on wheels,
Silly moments help us share how life feels.
When laughter's the fuel, we all stay aglow,
Our hearts light the way, helping kindness to grow.

So gather your giggles and share them around,
For light can be found where laughter is found.
Together, we'll dance in this jolly old park,
Igniting the world with our bright-hearted spark!

The Dance of Compassionate Souls

Two ducks in a pond, wearing tiny hats,
Twirl in a whirl, with the silliest chats.
They quack about rainbows, share tales from the sky,
While doing the tango, oh my, oh my!

A puppy in boots, leads the line with grace,
Spinning and hopping, in a fancy blue space.
All creatures unite, in this crazy old waltz,
With giggles and wiggles, no reason to halt!

A snail dropped a beat with a tap and a slide,
While a butterfly twirled and danced with great pride.
Together they laugh, as the grass sways and bends,
In a world where our dances can always make friends.

So let's jiggle and frolic, with spirits so full,
Embracing each tale, and the joy that's so cool.
For in every small wobble, a giggle's in sight,
A dance that brings hearts, to a giggling height!

Embracing Different Colors

A purple polka-dot with a green checkered tie,
Said to a blue stripe, 'You're one funky guy!'
They laughed through the rainbow, dancing with glee,
In a world full of hues, there's room for all three.

Orange and yellow made lemonade bliss,
While pink spotted kittens just couldn't resist.
They painted a canvas with shades of delight,
Creating a tapestry, a real colorful sight!

A fuchsia flamingo danced with a cow,
In wild boots and feathers, oh wow, oh wow!
With each little jiggle, the colors would meld,
In a joyful embrace, new friendships upheld.

So gather your palettes and dip in the fun,
Let's blend all our shades under this warm sun.
For in every splash, a story to tell,
Together we shine, making colors so well!

Blossoms of Brotherhood

In a garden, we plant silly seeds,
Laughter sprouts, just like the weeds.
Sharing smiles like candy bars,
Joy's aroma wafts from afar.

Tickle fights in the summer breeze,
High-fives exchanged with utmost ease.
Dancing squirrels join our parade,
Unity flourishes, none dismayed.

A pie-eating contest, what a sight!
Whipped cream missiles, oh what a fright!
Hand in hand, we form a chain,
Friendship grows, a sweet refrain.

Together, we wobble on a groove,
Finding rhythm, no need to prove.
In this merry land, all is well,
With giggles and glee, our hearts swell.

In the Shade of Kindness

Under an umbrella, we sip our tea,
Friendship served with a splash of glee.
Sunshine dances, shadows play,
Kindness blooms in a funny way.

A dog in sunglasses walks on by,
Chasing a cat with a well-timed sigh.
We share snacks, a picnic treat,
Each bite spreads joy, oh so sweet!

Jokes are shared under leafy greens,
Laughter echoes, bursting seams.
A parade of silliness, what a sight!
Together we giggle through the night.

With mischief in every corner found,
We swap our tales, the silliest around.
In this shade, all worries cease,
And together we cultivate our peace.

Canvas of Calm

With silly brushes, we paint away,
Doodles dance in a bright array.
Splashes of color, laughter in hues,
Creating a world with no bad news.

A canvas of giggles, oh what a sight!
Every stroke brings pure delight.
Painted smiles and quirky dreams,
In our gallery, nothing's as it seems.

Splatters of joy, with a wink and a nod,
Each frame a story, a friendly prod.
With every laugh, we add a new layer,
Creating a masterpiece, nothing could be fairer.

Here, brush in hand, we dream and create,
Masterpieces born from the light of fate.
In this artistic realm, we find our song,
Together, we revel, where we belong.

The Gentle Tides of Cooperation

On a beach of laughter, we build a fort,
Crafted from giggles, our favorite sport.
Waves of kindness crash at our feet,
Together we dance to a silly beat.

A sandcastle kingdom, big and wide,
Musical seashells, our joy can't hide.
Seagulls join in with their loud squawks,
As we share stories in playful talks.

Each grain of sand is a smile to share,
As we toss around our worries and care.
Bringing our quirks to this sandy place,
In every challenge, we find a chase.

Hand in hand, we ride the tide,
With room for laughter and love as our guide.
In this ocean of friendship, we glide with cheer,
Creating memories that forever endear.

Voices Merging in the Dawn

Birds tweet tunes in perfect sync,
While squirrels dance, with a wink.
The sun peeks, and smiles wide,
As laughter floats, like a joyful tide.

Pigeons strut like they own the street,
In funky hats, they skip and greet.
A chorus of giggles fills the air,
While daisies sway, without a care.

Sunbeams tickle the early dew,
Frogs croak jokes, it's quite the view.
A rabbit hops in stylish shoes,
Causing a stir, in morning hues.

With every chuckle, a new day starts,
As nature joins with happy hearts.
In this dance of life, we all belong,
Singing together, a joyful song.

The Bridge of Shared Aspirations

Two ants carry crumbs, side by side,
For a feast that's planned, with much pride.
An insect chef flips a tiny burger,
While butterflies cheer, getting a fervor.

A snail in a tie, takes the lead,
With a slow-motion crawl, planting a seed.
Raccoons gather, smartly dressed,
To discuss their dreams, feeling blessed.

The bridge they build is made of dreams,
With each shared joke, laughter beams.
A parade of critters, all in line,
United in goals, it's simply divine.

With colors bright, they paint the day,
In a whimsical dance, they dance and play.
For what's better than plans made with glee?
A bridge where all are bold and free.

The Symphony of Generous Hearts

In the meadow, a band strikes up,
With chipmunks clapping, and a turtle pup.
Each note is a giggle, each chord a cheer,
As the orchestra of joy draws near.

The bear on drums keeps a steady beat,
While beavers bring sticks, to make it neat.
A hedgehog sings in a scratchy tone,
Even the wind joins in, fully blown.

Foxes dance, twirling with flair,
While owls hoot harmonies, warm and rare.
They compose a tune that warms the night,
In this silly concert, everything's bright.

With every laugh, their hearts expand,
In this symphony, life is grand.
So join the fun, grab your part,
And play along with a generous heart.

A Collective Whisper of Kindness

Whispers mingle like honeybee swarms,
Spreading sweetness in playful forms.
A frog croaks softly, "You look great!"
While ladybugs flutter, don't be late!

The trees nod, their leaves a-shiver,
As they share tales that make hearts quiver.
A silver breeze carries warmth and cheer,
With giggles erupting from far and near.

Nutty squirrels share acorns galore,
While rabbits chuckle, then dance on the floor.
A secret language, giggles and grins,
In the hush of the morning, kindness begins.

So let's hold hands and whisper sweet,
In this light-hearted world, there's no defeat.
For in every giggle, camaraderie shines,
In this joyful hush, our laughter entwines.

Dawn of Collective Quietude

The sun peeks over the sill,
As neighbors fumble and chill.
Coffee spills on the lawn,
While cats chase a confusing dawn.

A squirrel steals crumbs like a thief,
In a dance that brings us belief.
We giggle at birds' silly tweets,
As breakfast chaos happily repeats.

Laughter bubbles with each spill,
As we sip tea and time stands still.
The garden blooms, a colorful fuss,
In the uproar, we find our trust.

So let the world spin out of control,
We'll share a laugh and a roll.
In the midst of our playful mess,
We sow joy, and that's our success.

Fragments of Shared Dreams

In a realm of mismatched socks,
We weave dreams from playful knocks.
A pillow fight ensues with glee,
As we toss fates like a confetti spree.

Our dreams collide, like silly hats,
In a circus dance with clumsy cats.
Laughter echoes in every room,
As we pull jokes from the dreamer's loom.

Around the globe with footed beds,
We glide on visions, bumping heads.
A shared giggle, a whispered scheme,
Turns ordinary nights into a dream.

Together we'll break the paper walls,
And catch the starlight as it falls.
In fragments we craft our quirky tune,
A marvelous dance to the moon.

Harmony in the Whispering Winds

The wind whispers secrets, oh so sly,
Tickling ears as it breezes by.
With giggles and puffs, it plays tag,
While trees sway in a joyful brag.

A wayward kite finds a friendly tree,
With a grumble from branches that once felt free.
A dance of leaves in a lighthearted tiff,
As clouds cartwheel, twist, and riff.

We laugh at the skies and their playful game,
As a shadowy puff shouts out a name.
Laughter ripples through nature's glee,
A ball of joy spins, just you and me.

Together we find our merry cheer,
In the light breeze, our worries disappear.
So float along with hearts unconfined,
As winds hum tunes, perfectly aligned.

Seeds of Serenity

Planting seeds of smiles today,
With humor's touch, in a silly way.
Each laugh a bud, each pun a bloom,
Turning gardens into a joyful room.

We dig our shovels in the ground,
With clumsy hands, we stumble around.
A worm does the cha-cha, what a sight!
As daisies dance in sheer delight.

With watering cans and cheerful screams,
We sprinkle the air with happy dreams.
Together we grace the earth with glee,
In this playful patch, we long to be.

So sow the seeds of joy and cheer,
In the plot of life, let's gather near.
With laughter and love, our care grows wide,
In the garden of humor, let joy abide.

Rippled Reflections

A pebble dropped in a pond, so round,
Causes giggles to dance all around.
Fish give a wink, a splash of delight,
Creating ripples that tickle the night.

Frogs join the fun, leaping with glee,
Croaking a tune, as silly as can be.
The water's a stage for laughter and cheer,
Where joy's a performer we all want to hear.

Someone lost their shoe, oh what a sight!
A duck takes a swim, it's quite a fright.
But in all the chaos, a truth we see,
The joy of the splash brings us all to be.

In rippled reflections, we find the key,
To bounce off each other, laughing with glee.
So let's drop our hearts, like pebbles in play,
And watch as the ripples brighten our day.

The Bridge Between Hearts

Two kids with ice cream, oh what a mix,
With sticky hands, and sweet little tricks.
They build a bridge made of laughter and fun,
Of jokes and sprinkles, oh, it's just begun!

A cat strolls by, with swagger so bold,
Dares all to cross, 'til the ice cream's sold.
With spritzers and giggles, they make it official,
A bridge of friendship, so sweet and superficial!

Paper boats sail, as the sun starts to fade,
While shadows and giggles in merriment wade.
With every little bump, they bounce off the beat,
Creating a path, just like ice cream in heat.

So let's build a bridge, with joy as our glue,
Made of candy and laughter, it's simple and true.
For hearts, when they connect, in this whimsical art,
Can bridge any gap, no matter how far.

Lanterns in the Night

In the dark of the night, comes a humorous light,
Balloons full of laughter, ready to take flight.
They wobble and jiggle, causing a scene,
Like jellybeans dancing in a flavor-filled dream.

With giggles as star dust, they float on and on,
Dreaming of sparkling till the first light of dawn.
But oh, what a ruckus, it's quite the delight,
When they bump into branches, oh what a fright!

A wise old owl joins in on the spree,
With a chuckle and wink, 'What an odd jubilee!'
He spreads laughter and peace, with feathers so bright,
These lanterns keep shining through the glorious night.

So let's hang our joys like lanterns aglow,
Casting warm shadows, letting friendship flow.
With humor as the fuel, we'll glitter and shine,
Lighting the world with a joy divine.

Choreography of Kindness

In a world where giggles play peek-a-boo,
Little acts of joy are the stars of the view.
With cha-chas and boogies, they dance through the day,
A hilarious rhythm, come join in the sway!

An ice cream truck rolls with a musical cheer,
Children groove to the tune, with no room for fear.
A sprinkle brigade, with giggling demands,
Creating a symphony from ice cream in hands.

With hugs as the steps, and laughter the beat,
We dance through our troubles, make kindness a treat.
From twirls in the park, to the jigs on the street,
We'll pirouette past worries, it's all quite a feat!

So loosen your shoes, let's enter the dance,
Where kindness and laughter create the romance.
In this silly ballet, our hearts find their home,
In a choreography of love, we shall roam.

Uniting Hearts in Harmony

In a world of giggles and quirks,
We find joy where laughter lurks.
A wink, a nod, a silly song,
Together we dance, it can't be wrong!

Juggling thoughts like clowns in a show,
We share our secrets, let chuckles flow.
A tickle here, a nudge over there,
Creating bonds that float in the air!

When troubles arise like pop-up clowns,
We chuckle, we grin, dismiss all frowns.
With every grin, our worries reduce,
In this circus of life, we find our truce!

So grab a friend, let silly reign,
We'll paint the world without any pain.
With jest and joy, let's make a plea,
To spread some fun, just wait and see!

The Bridge of Shared Dreams

We build a bridge with dreams quite goofy,
Like penguins in sweaters, oh how that's loopy!
A splash here, a jump there, watch us unite,
Crossing together, everything feels right.

With paper airplanes soaring high,
And gummy bears floating by,
We'll share our wishes and silly schemes,
United we stand in our wacky dreams.

A high five here, a wink and a grin,
We'll dance on the bridge, let the fun begin!
With laughter echoing like magical streams,
Our hearts entwined in the silliest teams.

So take my hand, let's stroll this way,
With giggles and dreams to brighten our day.
We'll celebrate life, one silly scream,
Together we laugh, crafting our theme!

The Melody of Gentle Voices

Whispers of laughter, soft as a breeze,
We sing our antics with the greatest ease.
Tickles of humor float through the air,
A symphony crafted with tender care.

Humming tunes of hiccups and snorts,
Our gentle voices bring light to all sorts.
With every note, we share a jest,
Creating a chorus that's simply the best!

We laugh like the sun peeking through the day,
In harmony's dance, worries fade away.
Let's strum on those feels, let our hearts rejoice,
For laughter's the melody, we proudly voice.

Join in the fun, make a sound or two,
Together our giggles will carry us through.
In this tune of nonsense, let's find our choice,
To gather and cherish our gentle voice!

A Tapestry of Connection

We weave our tales with threads of delight,
Each giggle a stitch, every smile so bright.
In this quilt of quirks, we find our grace,
A tapestry brightens every dreary space.

With yarns of laughter and sparkling dreams,
We quilt together, or so it seems.
A patch of kindness, a sprinkle of fun,
Together we craft, our hearts weigh a ton!

Watch the fibers twist as we blend,
In this jolly fabric, there's no end.
A pinch of absurdity, a dash of cheer,
We'll sew up the world, year after year.

So gather 'round, let's tie and sew,
In this playful dance, we'll let our love glow.
For in every stitch, a story we tell,
A quilt of connection, where all is well!

The Embrace of Shared Stories

Gather 'round, let's share a tale,
Of a donkey who danced without fail.
He tripped on a cat, oh what a sight,
The giggles erupted, hearts feeling light.

A frog wore a crown, claiming great bliss,
Said, 'Join my kingdom, you can't miss this!'
With laughter, we bonded, our voices soared,
In every odd story, peace was restored.

The turtle and hare, they opened a shop,
Selling smoothies that made you hop.
With each silly sip, we'd giggle and cheer,
In the land of pure fun, all worries disappear.

So tell me your story, I'll share you mine,
In the realm of oddities, we twinkle and shine.
With laughter as our glue, let's gather 'round,
In the embrace of our tales, true joy can be found.

The Path to Common Ground

Two squirrels met on a bustling street,
Each carrying acorns, a nutritious treat.
One dropped his stash, it rolled with a thump,
They laughed as it bounced, what a silly lump!

A raccoon stood guard, with a mask on his face,
Claiming he owned this particular space.
But they shared their snacks, and offered a truce,
Even critters know when to call a truce!

On this quirky journey, we all can unite,
Sharing our nuts, oh what a delight!
With whispers of kindness, we hop and we twirl,
Finding common ground in a whimsical whirl.

So let's join our forces, with laughter and cheer,
Creating a pathway, where all can draw near.
In the dance of the day, let our spirits abound,
On this merry adventure, we're all common ground.

The Warmth of Welcoming Arms

A bear in a hat called all for a hug,
With a grin of delight, his heart was so snug.
The hedgehog, confused, rolled in for a squeeze,
And they tumbled together, laughing, with ease.

A peacock spread feathers, a rainbow display,
Inviting all creatures to join in the play.
They danced in a circle, so silly and free,
A racetrack of joy, as wild as can be!

With wings and with paws, they shared in the fun,
Creating a circle that shone like the sun.
In each flippered embrace, and furry warm clasp,
The magic of friendship turned tension to rasp.

So the bear and the hedgehog, in laughter they sway,
With welcoming arms, they brightened the day.
For in every warm hug, a spark can ignite,
A dance of connection, a world feeling bright.

A Daydream of Accord

In a land made of candy, a dream took to flight,
Where licorice roads looped in pure delight.
A gumdrop parade led a jolly troupe,
With lollipop signs that yelled, 'Join the loop!'

A cotton candy cloud floated right by,
Singing sweet songs with a chocolate pie.
Each scoop of ice cream, a flavor so rare,
Brought strangers together, oh what a fair!

In this daydream, all troubles grew small,
As jellybeans danced, inviting us all.
With bubbles of laughter and breezes that play,
Creating a world where all could just sway.

So when life gets sticky, and you start to frown,
Remember the dream where love wears a crown.
In a burst of sweet laughter, let harmony ring,
For in sharing our joy, it's the best kind of fling!

The Language of Unity

In a world where we all chat,
Laughter is the best welcome mat.
When gestures speak louder than words,
We find joy, like singing birds.

Smiles exchanged like currency,
No need for fancy urgency.
When silly dances break the ice,
Unity feels oh so nice.

Bumping elbows, what a sight,
Why shake hands when you can fight?
Giggling friends from near and far,
Humor's our shining, guiding star.

In teasing jests, we find our way,
Building bridges, come what may.
With every laugh, we stitch the seam,
Creating a bright and shared dream.

Offerings of the Heart

From my kitchen, I share a pie,
Completely burned—oh my, oh my!
But smiles bloom like daisies fair,
Nothing like sweetness to show we care.

I made you soup, well sorta right,
The recipe lost its sense of sight.
Yet every spoonful, served with glee,
Whispers warmth as cozy as can be.

Jokes wrapped up like presents tight,
Unwrapping laughter brings delight.
A heartfelt gift, a belly laugh,
Peace spreads wide, like a friendly giraffe.

So let's gather, no need for fuss,
Together we thrive—oh, what a plus!
With funny tales and goofy cheer,
We offer love, year after year.

Umbrella of Kindness

Caught in a rain, we laugh and dance,
Kindness sprinkles like a happy chance.
Under the umbrella, we squeeze in tight,
Sharing stories till the morning light.

Raindrops fall, like peas in a pod,
Dancing splashes as we applaud.
Giggles echo, we leap and twirl,
In the storm, we have quite the whirl.

Let's catch a cab with hearts so bold,
When kindness sparks, magic unfolds.
With each warm nod, each silly grin,
Together we thrive—let the fun begin!

So grab your smiles and your best shoes,
With kindness we'll never lose.
Dance in the rain, splash it about,
In this lovely realm, there's no doubt!

A Path of Gentle Steps

Tiptoe through the daisies bright,
With cheesy jokes, we take flight.
Each step a giggle, each turn a grin,
 Inviting the world to join in.

Stumbling forward, whoops, we fall,
Laughter echoing—did you see that sprawl?
With every misstep, we wink and sway,
 The path of joy leads us away.

We skip and hop like playful deer,
 Learning to dance with no fear.
Gentle nudges, a shoulder's theatre,
 Making life a funny adventure.

So lace your shoes and come along,
 On this path where we all belong.
Through giggles and chuckles, we'll roam,
 Silly together, we find our home.

Rippling Spirit of Amity

In a town where all are nice,
Laughter echoes, not a vice.
They share their snacks and silly jokes,
Like wise old owls, not silly blokes.

The mayor dances with a pie,
While kids ride bikes and touch the sky.
A dog wearing shades joins the fest,
His wagging tail's the very best.

Neighbors whisper, 'Let's be pals!'
While sipping tea with friendly gals.
A funny hat upon her head,
A peace parade, it's well said!

In this land where giggles grow,
Balloons of joy in every row.
Let's throw confetti, feel the cheer,
With grinning faces, there's no fear.

Chorus of Gentle Souls

A chorus sings in perfect tune,
With melodies that lift the moon.
Songbirds tweet with humorous flair,
In harmony, they fill the air.

With jokes about a goat named Lou,
And dancing squirrels that love to chew.
Together they form quite a scene,
As rabbits prance, all fluffy and keen.

Each verse brings smiles; it's quite a sight,
Even grumpy cats can't help but bite.
They tap their paws to every beat,
Finding joy in life's silly sheet.

Joy is brewed in every note,
With dancing hats on every coat.
A clown explodes in colored glee,
In this joyful jamboree!

Mosaics of Forgiveness

In a patchwork quilt of bright delight,
Stitches hold what once was fright.
A cat and dog share a sunny spot,
Both claiming it, but forgetting the rot.

Silly squabbles fade away,
In a dance-off, they laugh and sway.
A turtle winks, then grabs a pie,
Flipping it high, oh my, oh my!

Children giggle, making amends,
With toys and snacks that hunger sends.
Handshakes filled with glitter and fun,
A truce declared when the day is done.

They paint their hearts with colors bright,
In a canvas of joy, day and night.
Each stroke a memory, laughter shines,
In this mosaic where love aligns.

Radiant Horizons

At dawn, the sun begins to smile,
With rays that dance and flirt awhile.
Balloons in sky, a colorful show,
Up they rise, to where? Who knows!

Whimsical critters gather round,
With playful banter, joy is found.
On this horizon, we share our dreams,
And burst out laughing, or so it seems.

A parrot jokes, 'I need a drink!'
While hippos pop and start to wink.
Dancing daisies sway in the breeze,
With buzzing bees that love to tease.

So, raise your glass to silly things,
To the joy and laughter that friendship brings.
In this light where fun never ends,
We're all just clowns, and that transcends!

Bonds Beyond Boundaries

We share a smile, it's quite contagious,
One wink can make the world outrageous.
With every laugh, the gap grows thin,
Who knew silliness could help us win?

In hats of daisies, we dance in line,
Two left feet make a comical sign.
Our quirks unite like jelly and jam,
Peace is the punchline; who knew it could slam?

From silly faces to goofy grins,
Each chuckle shoves away the sins.
The globe sways gently to our cheer,
Laughter is loud, but love is near!

So come on now, let's join the play,
In this circus of life, we'll find a way.
Bonds beyond borders, we'll craft our dance,
With humor and heart, we'll take a chance!

Radiance of Reconciliation

In mismatched socks, we'll start anew,
With rainbow ties and a bright pink shoe.
When quarrels fade with each silly joke,
The sparks of joy leave our hearts bespoke.

With cupcakes tossed and confetti burst,
We'll paint the town, laughing till we thirst.
Like bubblegum clouds that giggle and sway,
We'll mend our rifts in a playful way.

The sun shines brighter over our spree,
With every chuckle, we swim with glee.
A tickle here and a hug right there,
Reconciliation is far from rare!

So let's break the bread made of giggles,
As we wriggle, dance, and play with wiggles.
In the feast of joy, we'll find our place,
With laughter's warmth, we'll embrace grace!

The Language of Love

With silly gibberish and funny sounds,
We'll bridge the gaps all over towns.
A wink and a nudge, that's how we speak,
In the dialect of joy, we find the peak.

With ice cream cones and bubble-blowing,
Conversation flows like rivers glowing.
A tickle on the arm, a playful tease,
In this tongue of chuckles, our hearts find ease.

The words are fleeting, but the laughter grows,
A dance of kindness, everybody knows.
In goofy rhymes, our spirits soar,
A lexicon of joy, forevermore!

So gather 'round, let's cast our net,
In this language, we'll never forget.
Through giggles small, we'll conquer strife,
In the whimsy of love, we'll find our life!

Waves of Togetherness

Like waves of laughter splashing on sand,
Together we rise, united and grand.
With water balloons and splashes of fun,
Who knew unity could feel like a run?

We build our castles with giggles and cheer,
With every grain, we drop our fear.
The tide of joy pulls us closer still,
In this ocean of laughter, we find our thrill.

A synchronized dance on the shore so bright,
Two left feet making waves of delight.
When smiles crash like surf against the rock,
We'll ride together, tick-tock by tick-tock.

So let's surf the curls of laughter's embrace,
In every wave, we'll find our place.
Together we paddle, we row, we glide,
In this sea of joy, we'll take the ride!

The Embrace of Open Hearts

Let's share a smile, a goofy grin,
With open hearts, let joy begin.
A dance of laughter, a silly song,
In this big world, we all belong.

A cupcake here, a cookie there,
We sprinkle kindness everywhere.
With hug attacks and high-five flair,
We craft a bond beyond compare.

A tickle fight on a sunny day,
Bringing giggles that come out to play.
When friends unite with a wacky art,
Chaos ignites the open heart.

So let's all gather, no frowns allowed,
Celebrate life, make each other proud.
With silly hats and joyous chats,
We find our peace in fun-filled spats.

The Canvas of Life United

Life's like a canvas, bright and bold,
With splashes of colors, stories told.
A wobbly brush, oh what a sight,
We paint our dreams with pure delight.

In jigsaw pieces, we fit just right,
With laughs that giggle, shining so bright.
A splash of blue for trust's embrace,
Together we laugh, no need for grace.

Let's sculpt our joy with friendships tight,
In this goofy gallery, all feels right.
With silly poses and quirky style,
We create a world that makes us smile.

So come along now, let's blend our hues,
In the rhythm of life, we chase our views.
Together we giggle, we cheer and dance,
On this canvas of joy, we take our chance.

Melodies of Mutual Understanding

Two birds chirping a funny tune,
With silly notes that float to the moon.
We strum our hearts on a merry day,
In chords of laughter, we find our way.

A little jingle, a joyous hum,
With each new note, we all become.
A tickling harmony, we join in play,
Songs of togetherness light the way.

With tambourines and clapping hands,
We create a ruckus, no need for plans.
In every rhythm, we share our vibe,
With giggles and grins, we thrive, we jive.

So let's compose in this laughter spree,
A melody forged in harmony.
With every beat, we bridge the space,
Together in joy, we find our place.

Illuminating the Shared Path

We stumble together, trip on our feet,
With laughter as lanterns, our path can't be beat.
A shiny flashlight or sparkly glow,
Together we wander, wherever we go.

A compass of chuckles, we never lose sway,
With friends for a guide, brightening the way.
Through twists and turns, oh, what a ride,
With humor our fuel, we walk side by side.

We share our snacks under the moonlight,
With giggles so bright, we set wrongs right.
In this journey of joy, we lighten the load,
With playful hearts, we forge our own road.

So come take my hand, let's skip hand in hand,
In this funny adventure, oh isn't it grand?
With laughter as beacons, we chart our course,
Together we shine, our spirits a force.

www.ingramcontent.com/pod-product-compliance
Lightning Source LLC
Chambersburg PA
CBHW070319120526
44590CB00017B/2745